READING THE RIVER

Claudia Mauro

Library of Congress Catalog Card Number:
98-96754

Published in the United States of America
by Whiteaker Press
204 First Avenue South, Suite 3
Seattle, Washington 98104

ISBN 0-9653800-3-3

CONTENT

Acknowledgements iv

PART I

The Fine Art of Butch 2

Bashers' Lament 4

Getting Used to the Country 5

Lullaby for a Deep Blue Sea 6

Postcard from Second Mesa 7

At the Literary Festival 9

The October Moon Ambles
    Orange O'er the Mountains 10

The Opinion of Parrots 11

Keys 12

PART II

Tips for Romantic Types 14

Buddha of Self-Pity vs.
    Buddha of Self-Righteousness.................. 17

Snow 19

Love Poem for B 20

Invocation on Hudson Street 21

The Rapture 22

Figures of Speech 23

The Black Dress 24

Vigil 25

PART III

Start with Leaves 27

For a Seasonal Creek 28

Easter Poem for the Garden 29

September 30th 30

Secrets of Local Reception 31

Ascension 32

Owl 33

Reading the River 34

Then What Is this Thing Moving? 35

About the Author 37

Notes on Book Design 38

For Deborah Luecken

ACKNOWLEDGEMENTS

This work could not have been created without the generous support, commitment and love of the following people.

For my editor Shelley Tucker, the Mark McGwire of grammar, for her friendship, keen eye, generous commitment of energy and unwavering belief in this work.

For my dear friend and editor Lynn 'slash and burn' Garvey, for hanging in there with me through all the wrong metaphors, all the wrong spellings and all the wrong women, all these years.

For Tracy Lamb without whose brilliant design skills this book would be a loose stack of mimeographed pages tacked to a phone pole in the rain.

For Beejer Louise Whiteaker-Hawks—part elf, part angel, all butch.

For Ann Ready whose fine ear for language and impersonation of Mother Teresa in court shoes is a continuing inspiration to me.

PART ONE

The womanly art of being butch—is the ability to pass yourself
off as exactly yourself. This is done primarily by identifying
and then eliminating the difference between what you say and
what you do. That difference, (between what you say and what
you do, what you love and what you embrace), equals roughly,
who you are. Eliminate that difference, and voila—you
are yourself.

To be butch you must wear your weather in your walk, open
shoulder and sure hip. A butch knows her scars are beautiful.
They are the proof she needs of a grace unseen that knits the
wound between who she loves and who she forgives. A butch
has no ability to pass (either way), and has lost the desire
to do so.

This is what she knows about fear—we all die in battle
whether or not the life we live is our life.

To be butch you must stop apologizing to strangers for
lingering too long among the living parts of the world.
Because like all women, you can try to be a good girl,

but you can never be good enough. This is why a butch laughs with her mouth and thighs open. She is the out loud poem.

A butch does not argue the relevance of gender between women, whether this is passé or has cachet. (In fact, she rarely speaks French at all.) She especially does not argue this with a femme, knowing it will annoy them both and waste time that could have been spent appreciating how three inch heels accentuate the grace lines of a calf in silk. If gender must be discussed, she does so only with a big, sissy, nelly boy, who like her, cannot pass.

A butch lives in exile from a country that does not exist. Her body is her only home, her voice, one whole nation. To be butch you must understand the power of words, and refuse to let your heart be murdered by adjective. You must know the value of story and carry a library in each clear eye. The fine art of butch is to take your seat at the fire and unfold your own story—then toss it in, to rise as heat and light.

How you must envy
The faggot boys
Whose bones you break

Leaving them to weep
So tenderly
In one another's arms

I have a habit of deadbolts.
Even way out here, a lock is like a cigarette,
something a woman can do
against what wants inside.

But tonight dark wants a witness,
so the door stands open and
midnight bangs on its hinges.

The moon walks in.
Her light is broken in a roadside ditch.
She says, "Some things are lost,
some stolen—what about you?"

It's late.
Wind and the cedars begin to sweep up.
Frogs count out the time
in silver black cadence.

When they opened my legs
I saw the picture cut from a book
tacked to the ceiling in four points,
two women at the seaside, the turn of the century.
high collars, bustled to their shoetops,
whalebone corsets laced abdomens tight.
Their expression was serene.
Valium drifted with the saline.
The flatline hum of florescents sounded like the ocean.
We all stared out to sea.

You were a slow bubble rising through the picture,
and back then you could have been anything—
a dolphin, an otter with your ten week tail.
I was the female carapace scraped along the beach, leaving
trace amounts and tracklines tattooed in the sand.

The silver needle with its spurt of silver thread
sewed the cervix to sleep. Then the women's work—
vacuuming, cleaning, bleeding, wiping up,
piece work, the cannery line.

This is for the still mornings
when you tack your little boat
near the rim of my opening eye.
A story in a bottle, a lullaby,
some quiet rhyming song,
for metal spoons and whalebones—
how they split
the deep blue sea and dawn.

Mr. Hill,
from Massapequa Park,
was my teacher at Patchogue elementary school.
He taught us fourth graders that way out west
there was a group of Indians named Hopis,
whose language had no future tense.

They had been around awhile
but died out because white settlers
could not teach them to farm corn.
The white people tried but
they couldn't understand
how a seed grew.

Believe me,
this is the kind of thing you remember
when you're desperate
for a future tense.

Those early American summers
we floated around Shinnecock Inlet in a borrowed boat.
Some kids swam in Lake Ronconkoma but not us.
My grandmother crossed herself at the name.
Strange Indian legends (that somehow made their way
into Italian) about underwater seeps and angry ghosts
waiting to drown the thick-limbed daughters of immigrants.

And we did drown there regularly.

Maybe the ghosts just wanted somebody to talk to,
whispering a dead language into sinking ears.

But I don't think it was the ghosts' fault.
I think it has something to do
with the weight of a native tongue—
hauling it around in your head.
Something about being unspoken
and trying to swim.

A pregnant woman
>   patiently waits while

> a young girl pretends
> at being a butterfly

She emerges from the ladies room
>   running backwards

THE OCTOBER MOON AMBLES
ORANGE O'ER THE MOUNTAINS

My trusty editor accuses me
of loving pretty lines too well.

She says,
"It always seems like there's something...immense,
just under the sentiment."

She's right, of course.

Over our evening tea,
   wind and October light shift their weight,
      the sky tips a little—

(That's a pretty line, don't you think?)

She goes home. I go to my apartment.
She goes to bed with her lover.
I won't go near the bed.

I watch the October moon sidle up
my picture window. Together
we peek under the pretty lines.
When our eyes meet
neither of us says a word.

God made us to fly
this brilliant color around—
a little present for sky.

We know that
but it attracts the wrong kind
of attention and God
is easily (obviously) distracted.

So they put us in comfortable boxes
and give us fat words to eat.
They all want to be heard.
They all want to talk
about flying.

Say you realize your keys are not
where you thought and the search begins
of your usual absent minded haunts.

These are dangerous times.

Reaching around shelves
of dark possibilities,
the formerly friendly credenza
turns inquisitor—full of books
you pretend to read, rotting
poems and payments due.

Evidence of your shiftless neglect
licks a blind fingertip and skitters
for the deeper dark.

Don't look for divine intervention.
God's been off searching whole galaxies
for the pencil behind his ear,
the glasses on his head.

And don't try to reason it out.
That can send you teetering
around for hours open-mouthed
like a bat hoping to get lucky.

Some people
consistently lose everything.
Once I had a lover
who finally found her keys in the freezer.
I haven't seen her for years.

Part Two

A wall you can see through
is not necessarily a wall you can walk through.

If they tell you,
"In two years I will perform a miracle"—
have them call you in two years.

Her forgotten handkerchiefs
and socks (nestled in their cozy little pairs) will taunt you.
The design of deepest grief *is* laundry.

Gravity is a mean drunk.

For your love match, avoid conspiracy theorists.
Imaginary rats have the sharpest teeth.

The devil manipulates through logic.

Love may be blind, but it can drive.
Never leave your keys where your
clitoris can find them.

The leap of faith and the flying fuck
are similar, yet eerily different.

An illusion with a 2x4 can crack you
over the head as good as a train wreck.

Remember—order creates peace,
not truth, not justice, just peace.

Who you take to bed at three in the afternoon
and who you want there at three a.m.
are different matters entirely.

Never eat a pomegranate on your first date.

The inability to hold a contradiction
makes lying a necessity.

Light sees what it wants to see, but
darkness will meet you anywhere.

A truth about heartbreak—
It's not that you can't forget her,
it's that you will.

The most violent thing
either of you will ever say is
"I love you."

A Quiz—
Test Your Love Savvy

1. Which of the following mythic personalities
   best describe you and your intended? Be honest.
   Which best describe your intentions?
   Mix and match:
       a. Icarus   Daedalus
       b. Isis   Osiris
       c. Demeter   Hades
       d. Maris   Mantle
       e. Wiley Coyote Roadrunner

2. The distance between two sleeping
   bodies pressed together is:
       a. The unnameable loneliness.
       b. The exact dimension of your collective shadow.
       c. The specific gravity of: (grief) x (X/Y)
                      where X = an X
                      and Y is a hopeless question.
       d. Maybe the walls are sleeping and the lovers
           are a dream cast along with their shadows.
       e. A body in motion tends to remain in motion.

3. True or False—
         This whole road is rigged in circles.
         What you turn away from you turn into.
         It's an outrage. All that leaving for nothing.

4. Fill in the blank—
         At the center of your heart is a river.
             Its name is _____*.*

BUDDHA OF SELF-PITY VS.
BUDDHA OF SELF-RIGHTEOUSNESS

She makes it perfectly clear.
It's not what I do or say
but who I am—
that old unloved, insoluble problem.

Restating the whole world's obvious opinion
is a burden but her compassion is great.
The door slams by accident. She forgets
to take her compassion with her.

My deadlines come and go
but her compassion lingers.
I used to take it everywhere.
Now I don't go anywhere.

That damn compassion's grown too fat
and we can't get down from upstairs.
Nothing to do but sit and watch
nature shows on the television.

Compassion and I stuff pretzels down my gullet
tubs at a time and contemplate my navel—
the hulking sag of it, my waist of meat.

Inside the fuzzy screen,
a sooty little bird bangs its sooty little head
against a brick chimney and pries gritty
morsels from the mortar with its beak.
We couldn't agree more. This is quite a dharma
we've got ourselves around here.

That autumn evening
      your clothes fell
           open

The moon took you
    in her smooth hands

  You glistened

a sound like falling snow

That kiss
    a firefly cupped
        in the palms

A master taps marble and it appears the mountain itself
folded the still supple Christ into his tender mother's lap.

Love like that is an open wound, blood and river mixed.
I suppose that's how we're born from stone into dusty color.

How every morning this world is given and given,
and how for a time, the buddhas did not recognize themselves.

Inside your hand there's a hammer made of moonlight and wind.
That's what I mean when I call you beautiful.

How many ways can I say this?
The body waiting in rock. Your fingertips falling as rain.

Dear god of little things, of ordinary things
    of missing buttons and Tuesdays
        of meadowlarks and river clover
            consider us.

Here is the simple arc of our lovers body
        nestled in dream above the June morning,
            tender ship, tiny song.

Mindful god of clocks and moth wings
    house sparrows and window latches,
        There are dandelions in the broken sidewalks
            along Hudson Street who know your
                footsteps by heart.

Like everything, we have nothing.
    Don't wake us. Leave us in this easy weave
        of breath over bone. Fold us up
            in your book of days.
        Say our name once and forget us.

Another winter
Then desire touched grace
And whispered
Now

You say
There is something in me
  that is me

I say
A woman's body in moonlight
  is proof enough of God

We are three, then none
The exquisite pulse takes form
Leaves our clothes lying empty
              we're gone

My beloved arrives
wearing nothing but
a fright wig and running shoes.
Only the tea kettle screams.
We talk, all
malaprop and maxim—

"A bird in hand does not fear the butcher's cat."

"Casters roll your bed upon the waters."

*"A nod is as good as a wink
to a blind highway, etc."* Who cares?

Somebody get the damn tea kettle
before it melts to its element.

Where a lover's hands
   once pulled silk above
      the heat of her thighs—
   now two cautious crows
      squabble in the fog.

  One says—
It was a game of twigs the wind took.
Come, let's chase another shiny lie.

But the other falls in love
  with the rising moon and
    can't look away
  from her cool absence
   filling room after empty room.

I move on,
learn to let go.
But the body, poor dog,
waits for your key in the lock.

"Come to sleep," I tell her
"She's never coming back."

She turns wooden circles
on the bed but will not lie.
"Look," I tell her,
"Stars move."

All night she watches them
while headlights sweep
the bedroom walls.

PART THREE

Start with leaves
the way they bear the unbearable
mercy of late April rain.
Then describe this newborn
morning for the hungry animal it is.

You've learned to warm your bed with stones,
to get by on whatever passion you've put up
for the long winter your life has become.

But now this fragrance, this pliable light.
The leaded window pushes open,
to a clear bowl of swallows.
It hurts to hope this much—
the bones of birds are hollow.

Where do you begin?
Now that you know what hope can do
to the soft wood of the body.

What secret word does dirt spell out
to coax each replaceable face to light?

How do you start?
Now that you know there's no safe distance
between the searing bud and its casual release.

Truth be told
  in summer
I missed your voice.

A wobbly twig
  caught in a whirlpool.
    All day the moment repeats itself.

Mergansers are forever scribbling
  their mornings across the surface of the cove.

A field mouse pauses in a thicket
  then brambles along at the rain's pace.

In the cloud language,
    chapel still means creek.

One packet of letters
  is insufficient to form a fluid world.

We should learn to spell with pebbles,
  an alphabet of twigs and salamanders
    drawn into the palm.

I'll choose
  24 stars glinting
    in the tiny river's face.

In the mud religion
that worms enjoy
each epiphany of cabbages
and resurrection of the daffodils
asks for nothing. What lays fallow, lies
and proof becomes the world.

Swallows again,
quoting the air with affable swoops,
recite a local gospel according to trees.

You can believe nothing.
Though saints have tended them
sanctity is not elemental to squash.
Oblation will not move the turnips.

If it's ritual you're after—
Pick a rising moment
and be the ancient story.
The garden gate is narrow—
you can always enter here.
Plant each foot with some
plain kindness and live.
Just live.

The wind
   casually mentions
  something about winter

The sun wanders idly by

I have to stop writing
  The north wind is tapping
    the bottom of my right foot

I'm going to see
  what it wants

Listen—
it may sound like the perfect apple
but nobody wants to swallow the sanctimonious worm.

We are all quite capable of making
our own breakfast, thank you very much.

The neighborhood birds—
worm aficionados all, strike up
an impromptu apple tree orchestra
at precisely five.

A crow wobbles
along a rusty rooftop antenna
and dines on something truly nasty.
Another crow shows up, cranks out
a few bars of crow language
and they fly off together.
The empty antenna shimmies
and squeaks out a few notes.

It was a clear morning,
the cove a perfect mirror of sky.
A butterfly caught in the water,
trapped in her reflection.

Five times her paper wings heaved
and beat with such a buzz of fury,
that her reflection nearly released her,
but each time thin wings collapsed
and sank deeper in the cool water.

The cove gently rocked her.
When all was lost, a kingfisher
dove from a madrona and
skimmed her from drowning.

Together they rose into the sky.
A ripple of widening circles fanned out,
then settled. For a moment the sky trembled.

Listen

What words want
　is to be opened,
　to be born
　whole.

　　The word

　　　OWL

can become itself
　and sweep this page home.

Words want that
　　　chance at a chance.

When darkness spoke its bright hunger—
　　　it woke into light.

Rain believes in circular theology
Rocks opt more for the steady state
but both agree, even a river begins.

A drop of rain remembers something,
and the world is full of rivers.

This is a slow conversation.

But if you're willing to wait a long time,
any river rock can recite a time before the forge
when all our tongues were molten.

In your eyes rain can see
that same terrible hope of her own
clear tumble through light.

THEN WHAT IS THIS
THING MOVING?

Horses in a field

      soft rain

Canyon wren's
    nine note
        descending
           song

Above the river
      slow mist

    Swallows
      in the open air

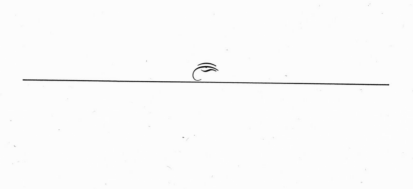

Claudia Mauro is, among other things, a first generation New York Italian Amazon leather Buddhist butch in recovery. She holds Federal Aviation Administration commercial pilot certificate number 131407693, and certainly knows how to stall, and how to recover.

She has been employed as an Alaskan bush pilot, merchant mariner, street junkie, fisheries science technician, hypnotist and computer programmer.

She currently writes and teaches in Seattle, Washington and occasionally moonlights as a pilot in Southeast and Western Alaska.

Her goal is to embody the sacred, the profane and the moment they ride in on.*

*As always, these final prepositions are dedicated to Shelley.

Book cover is 80 lb. Encore Dull Cream Cover with a matte varnish. Inside stock is Simpson Evergreen Recycled. All paper used is 100% recycled.

Cover and inside text were set in Futura Condensed Light, AGaramond, and Wood Ornaments. AGaramond is a recasting of Garamond, originally designed in the 16th century by Claude Garamond. The new Adobe AGaramond was redesigned by Robert Slimbach in 1989. The Wood Ornament font was developed in 1990 by the Adobe Type Design Team using research from 19th century industrial styles of wood block prints.

Book design by Tracy Lamb, Seattle, Washington.

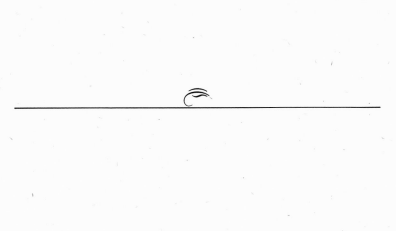

TO ORDER BOOKS BY WHITEAKER PRESS

Reading the River, by Claudia Mauro, 50 pages. At once sensual and deeply spiritual, this work welcomes the reader and shows why Mauro is rapidly becoming a favorite in women's poetry. $13.95 per book

Stealing Fire, Writings by Claudia Mauro, 50 pages. Exquisite poems and stories guide you on a profoundly spiritual journey through the wilderness of the human heart. $12.95 per book

Openings, Quotations on Spirituality in Everyday Life, 92 pages, Inspiring quotations by women and men. Shelley Tucker, editor. $14.95 per book

Animal Tails: Poetry & Art by Children, 84 pages. Poems and art on animal themes by children, ages 4-12. Shelley Tucker, editor. $14.95 per book

Name _____ Date _____

Street Address_____ Phone_____

City _____ State _____ Zip_____

E-mail _____

BOOK TITLE	PRICE	QUANTITY	AMOUNT
Stealing Fire	12.95		
Openings: Quotations on Spirituality	14.95		
Animal Tails: Poetry & Art by Children	14.95		
Reading the River	13.95		
Washington state residents please add 8.2% sales tax			
Shipping and Handling $2.50 for first book plus .50 each add'l book			
TOTAL			

Please make checks payable and mail to: Whiteaker Press
204 First Avenue South, Studio 3
Seattle, WA 98104
E-mail: cmauro1@aol.com
1-800-489-9095